FREEDOM FROM DEPRESSION

By Curry R. Blake

General Overseer

John G. Lake Ministries

and

Dominion Life

International Apostolic Church

Copyright © 2012 by Curry R. Blake
All Rights Reserved

Published by
CHRISTIAN REALITY BOOKS
P.O. Box 742947
Dallas TX 75374
1-888-293-6591

Cover Design by Pyrolab Designs.

Unless otherwise noted, all Scripture quotations are taken from the King James Bible.

This book or parts thereof may not be reproduced in any form without express written permission of Curry Blake.

The teachings in this book were taken from sermons given by Curry R. Blake on 7/22/12.

Printed in the United States of America.

Dedication

I dedicate this book: "Freedom From Depression" to my earthly Dad and Mom, Johnny Frank Blake and Johnnie Faye Blake.

While I experienced many things as a child, both good and bad, I do not remember hearing either of them ever tell me that I could not achieve something. On the contrary, they both constantly reinforced in me that I could do whatever I put my mind to. They never called me names as I have heard other parents do. They celebrated my victories and consoled me in my failures.

I spent the last week of my Dad's life with him. For the last 20 years of his life he took great pleasure in the choice I made for my life's direction. His last words to my mother concerning me were, "You know, I believe Curry does have the gift."

My mother always encouraged me concerning God's calling on my life. She constantly reminded me of the fact that God spared my life and healed me, and that she dedicated me to Him as a 17-month-old child.

Their positive outlook and input into my life helped protect me from the depression that I have seen in so many people, especially ministers.

Curry R. Blake

TABLE OF CONTENTS

How to Beat Depression 1

Replacing Fear with Faith 33

HOW TO BEAT DEPRESSION

Statistics say that more than 35 million Americans suffer from depression. One of the things that we've noticed is that no war is usually won as a single battle. Usually, wars are a long list of battles. The side that wins the most battles, or the most important battle, is the one that actually wins the war.

There are times when a person or a nation may go through a war, and one battle or one event can turn the tide. For instance in World War II, along with the Allies, we basically defeated Germany in Europe. We all then moved into the Pacific and went against Imperial Japan. The main reason that the Pacific Theater of the war was actually won was because the will of the Japanese people was defeated. It was because of dropping one bomb. It wasn't a lot of battles; it was one bomb that turned the will of the people.

Going back to the United States, our soldiers did not lose the Vietnam War. It was actually lost due to the will of the people and to the will of the politicians. The two primary reasons for the loss of the Vietnam War were politicians and the United States colleges. Those two things were why that war was brought to an end as it was.

The Vietnam War was the first war where we actually had a live footage where people actually saw what was going on. Because of that, people lost the will to fight. Our soldiers did a good job. Our soldiers never lost a single battle, per se, in the

Vietnam War, but it was the will of the people and the will of the politicians that actually turned the war.

The key is to turn the will of the people. That's exactly what happened with the bombing of Hiroshima and of Nagasaki. Since it turned the will of the people, it was not a military victory in that sense.

The reason I'm saying that is because many times in a war, you go through many battles. Some of the battles you tend to win and some you lose. The idea is not to lose any battles.

We're promised as Christians that we do not have to lose battles. I want to emphasize this. Many times, when you're in a battle, you may suffer what we would think of as a defeat or a setback. The key to being an overall winner is to be the one who can get back up and regain initiative. One of the key points in spiritual warfare is that many times you're moving forward and you have momentum, and then a setback will take place. What matters is whether or not you have the will to continue to regain the initiative. If you lose the initiative on the battlefield, you must regain it. That's just a primary key. Again, regaining the initiative has to do more with your will. It has to do with you continuing. You have to decide to continue.

One of the things that I've noticed in teaching is that we have a tendency to want to throw everything on the devil. Understand that the devil is behind everything, but there are things that you can do, things that you can address, and take care of. You can create a defense against the devil.

I was blessed to be with Dr. Lester Sumrall for many years. He used to do a teaching called, "How to Cope," in which he dealt with how to cope with depression, divorce, grief, or anything else you can name.

I want to show you how to beat your biggest enemy, which is fear. We have had teachings on fear, and this lesson is a take off on those. I want to show you how to defeat depression.

First of all, I'll give you some medical statistics. I'm not saying they are truth. They are true, but they're not truths. There's a big difference. The Word of God is Truth. The statistics may be true statistics, but they are not the Truth. They are only statistics.

The word "fear" is used over 400 times in the Bible. Now, by contrast, the word "faith" is only used 247 times in the Bible. Out of that 247 times, it is only used 2 times in the Old Testament. In the New Testament there are over 245 instances of the word "faith."

In Proverbs 12:25, there is a Scripture that says,

> 25 Heaviness in the heart of man maketh it stoop: but a good word maketh it glad.

That's the King James Version. The New King James Version says,

> 25 Anxiety in the heart of man causes depression, But a good word makes it glad.

Did you hear that? "Anxiety in the heart of man causes depression." The second part of the verse says, "…but a good word makes it glad."

The Bible says, "In the last days men's hearts will fail them for fear of what is coming upon them." A lot of that has to do with anxiety. It can be all kinds of things, not just end time things. You can almost see it taking place on a daily basis. There are also aspects of economic collapse. In the home mortgage collapse, people are losing their homes. A lot of people are losing their jobs. All of these different things bring anxiety.

A person can suffer anxiety for a short period of time. A lot of people do that, and it's not necessarily that detrimental. It becomes detrimental when it stays for days, weeks, months, or sometimes even years. We're going to look at more specifics on this.

Notice: depression is not just a mood swing. Remember that. It's not merely a fluctuation of emotions. One day you're up, and the next day you're down. Your mood fluctuates, and most of that has to do with what goes on around you in your immediate environment. You can feel up, you can feel down, you can feel up, you can feel down; it's that kind of thing. Those things usually last a day or so; that's somewhat normal.

God made us a three-fold being: spirit, soul, and body. Our soul has emotions, and in these emotions, we were meant to have a wide range of emotions. We were meant to be able to experience grief. I'm not saying that grief is a part of what God wants you to experience, but you were built so that could experience it. It shows how you can experience the wide range of emotions; you have a spectrum of emotions.

Notice that clinical depression may last weeks, months, even years. When it goes on for that length of time there's a reason for it. It is a specific problem, so we want to talk about that.

How To Beat Depression

Depression in the United States is on the rise, more so than it has ever been. As a matter of fact, people born after 1950 are actually ten times more likely to experience depression than the generation before it. These are the statistics.

If you're not in depression, don't get in depression just because you hear the statistics, and they say that you are supposed to be depressed. Stay out of depression. People between the ages of 25 and 45 are the ones who are most likely to suffer from depression.

Adolescents have the fastest growth rate for depression. Think about that. That in itself is just a shame, because childhood should be happy. Young people shouldn't be going through depression, but you see more and more of it. We'll talk about some reasons for it a little later on.

Another statistic is that women are twice as likely to experience depression more so than men. Part of that could be because depression has a lot to do with emotions, and women tend to be more emotional. Women are more sensitive in certain areas, so they tend to dwell on things a little longer than men generally do.

More statistics say that 35 million Americans, a little over 16% of the population, will require treatment for depression at some point in their lives.

At any given time, there are 13 to 14 million Americans that are clinically depressed. I keep using that word clinical depression; that's a good definition.

Clinical depression is distinct in that the symptoms are so severe that they disrupt lives. It gets so bad that they cannot even carry on their average daily routine.

There are other aspects of depression. Besides clinical depression, there's also something called dysthymic disorder. It is chronic, low-grade depression. In other words, it's always there, it's not too severe and doesn't interrupt your daily activities, but you are always depressed and always melancholy.

Then there's another aspect of depression, which a lot of people don't think of as depression. It used to be called manic-depression, but now we have a new term for it, and its called bipolar disorder. That's a branch or a type of depression.

Bipolar disorder is characterized by periods of euphoria. In other words, you're just ecstatic, you're happy, you're up, everything's good, but then it's contrasted by periods of severe depression. In other words, you hit these peaks, and then it takes a dive. A person can be feeling really good, everything can be great, and then in a split second they're back down.

We're going to talk about the purposes and causes of these things. I'm going to show you two-fold, and it's not always either one or the other. One usually affects the other and causes the other. Science only looks at one. We're going to look at both.

>1. You have mental causes.
>
>2. You have demonic causes.

If it is demonic, then it is a demon influence, which tries to bring a spirit of depression, which is usually also a spirit of fear. This spirit of fear tries to come upon you, it gets you to thinking, and it gives you suggestions. You start to dwell on the negative, on the bad. Then it gets you to dwell on future possible bad, not the reality bad. In other words, it gets you to think what could happen. You think, "This could be bad," or "That's going to turn out bad." It's almost always in the future.

Worry is almost always future. Seldom is it just right now, in front of you. People spend a lot of time worrying about the future and worrying about problems saying, "Oh, we're going to lose our house. We're going to fall on hard times." Well, you haven't lost your house yet. Trust in God. Put your faith in God. Keep your mind on God. Go after God. Don't put your faith in the future and worry.

I want you to realize that a demonic oppression can come upon you. Dr. Sumrall used to say that there were seven steps or levels of demonic possession. They just start with regression and all of these other areas until they actually reach full-fledged possession. The enemy gets hold of you and is able to influence you to different degrees.

The first key is to keep your mind guarded against even letting him get a foothold.

Realize this: the enemy can come upon you, and he will suggest things to you. The enemy can't do a lot to you. He has to suggest things to you that you then buy into. He will suggest a negative thought, a future fear, a future worry, and get you to dwell on that thing.

In Proverbs 23:7 it says that what you think about you become.

> 7 For as he thinketh in his heart, so *is* he: Eat and drink, saith he to thee; but his heart *is* not with thee.

When you think about something for a period of time, you start creating pathways for it in the neurons of your brain. The neural pathways in your brain begin to form a way of thinking; you actually create a pattern of thinking. The more you think on it, the more it gets engraved in your brain. The more you think on it, the deeper the engraving gets, and the easier it is for you to get into the rut of thinking like that. Again, what the enemy usually attacks is your mind.

The enemy might attack your body instead. You might have some type of pain and, immediately when you have that pain, he will try to give you a thought of what that pain might be. "Well, that's probably a heart attack," or "That's probably cancer." He will hit you with a pain that is nothing but just a pain, and then he'll try to hit you with a thought. He will get you to thinking on the possibility of you having cancer or the possibility of you having a heart attack. He will get your mind into the rut of thinking like that.

What happens physiologically is that the enemy will give you a thought, and then you buy into that thought. Jesus said in Matthew 6:28, "Why take ye thought..." Usually, when you get a thought, you will take that thought, and you will talk about it,

or you will think about it, or you will dwell upon it, or mediate upon it.

Meditating on fear or a possible problem is called worry. When you worry, you are meditating upon the negative. However, when you meditate upon the Word of God, you meditate upon the goodness of God and the faithfulness of God. I would say that it is not just that you have the potential to overcome, but there is the probability that you will overcome.

The enemy will try to give you a thought, you will think about it, and what you think about, you will start to become. What happens when you think about it is that certain chemicals are released in your brain. If you think about a funny story, you will start laughing. You could be in a certain mood or have a certain attitude, but then, when someone mentions a funny scene out of a movie or a funny joke, you'll start laughing. You might even tell yourself a joke, and then laugh at it. When you do that, it releases endorphins into your body. Those chemicals are released from the activity of the brain and go throughout your body, bringing it to health. That's the reason the Bible says in Proverbs 17:22,

> 22 A merry heart doeth good *like* a medicine: but a broken spirit drieth the bones.

By your thoughts, you can actually create in yourself the positive state of being, both physically and mentally. By the same token, if you think negative, if you think on the fear, or if you think on a possible future problem, you are releasing negative chemicals throughout your body. That's why they say that bipolar disorder is simply a chemical imbalance. Well, it is a chemical imbalance. The problem is that the medical community thinks that the chemical imbalance is the problem when it's not—it's a result of the problem.

When I say the enemy, I am talking about the devil himself, demons, or any adversary that is a spirit being that is against man. Any adversary like that, any demonic spirit coming against man, is the initial problem. Then, as he brings these thoughts to you, you grab hold of them, and your brain starts to release negative chemicals. Why? That's because you're thinking too much about the wrong thing. That's what makes it a chemical imbalance.

If you think about good things, you can have a chemical imbalance in a good way. Think about good things, and think about what the Bible says.

Philippians 4:8,

> 8 Finally, brethren, whatsoever things are true, whatsoever things *are* honest, whatsoever things *are* just, whatsoever things *are* pure, whatsoever things *are* lovely, whatsoever things *are* of good report; if *there be* any virtue, and if *there be* any praise, think on these things.

It says that whatever is true, whatever is just, whatever is pure, and whatever is of good report, think on these things. If you do that, you will have a chemical imbalance, but it will be a good chemical imbalance. It will release good things, good endorphins, into your body. It will create a state of health within your body. That too, is a chemical imbalance—but it's a good one.

On the other hand, if you think on the negative, if you think of the problems, and if you think of every possible future problem that could be, that releases negative hormones (negative chemicals) into your body. That creates a negative/bad chemical imbalance. That's where all of that comes from.

The good thing is that if you come to me about a disease of some sort, I'm going to minister to you. I'm going to command that thing to go. I'm going to command your body to be healed. I'm going to break any of the power of the enemy. We can get you well. It is that simple. It is a truth. It is a fact of the Bible. It's a fact in our life and in our experience that we can get you well.

You can go right back out and get sick again. My praying for you is not going to make you immune. You know that you can come to me because of some disease. Let's say that you have kidney failure. I will pray for you, and God will heal you. When you go back out, that does not make you immune to future kidney failure.

Prayer and ministry are not creating immunity; it's not like an inoculation against something. It is simply setting you free. You can go back out, and get it all over again.

You can come to me and say, "I have lung cancer, because I smoked cigarettes." I can pray for you, and God will heal your lung cancer. You can go back out, start smoking again, and get lung cancer all over again. You can do that because ministry does not create immunity.

It is the same with depression. We can cast that thing out, or we can break the spirit of fear. Fear is where depression comes from. It starts with a spirit of fear that comes and attaches itself to you. The way it attaches is that it has to suggest something negative or something bad to you. It might be a possible outcome of some future event. You will decide to take that thought by dwelling upon it, by meditating upon it.

I can get that spirit of fear off of you, but if you don't change the way you think, nothing is going to change. I can set you free, but you can go right back out, and if you don't change your pattern of thinking, you will become depressed again. You will get right back into it. Why? That's because prayer and ministry are not inoculations for depression. That is not what ministry is.

Like I said, we can cast that thing off of you, but if you don't change the way you think, then you will still be creating negative hormones, negative chemicals, that go into your body, causing a negative or bad chemical imbalance.

This is where psychosomatic diseases or psychosomatic illnesses come from. *"Psychosomatic"* means *mind over body*. Basically it means that you're using your mind to destroy your body. Positive minded, upbeat people don't get psychosomatic diseases. Psychosomatic diseases are almost always a result of the people who get into a state of depression or constantly meditate upon the negative.

Some of the characteristics of depression come upon people who are subject to things such as anger, rejection, or family issues. These things can come from divorce, abuse, failure, fear of failure, or just fear, itself. It can cause hopelessness. It can bring depression and lack of control over a person's own life.

If you think that you don't have control over your own life, then you might go into depression. Grief, loss, guilt, or shame can bring depression. Loneliness, isolation, negative thinking, destructive mindsets, or even stress in itself can set these things off and can cause depression. You'll notice that all of these things that I have brought up here are negative type influences.

A persistent state of depression will change the chemical makeup in your body. In other words, if you constantly think negative thoughts, you will create a negative situation within your body through the chemicals released into your body. In those cases, it's not that we're casting out a devil, but we may need to break the devil's assault, the attack against you. Notice what I say: "A persistent state of depression will change the chemical balance in mind and body."

Many times, if you're staying depressed or staying down, it might be because you're always worried and thinking about the negative things. It's not about breaking the power of the devil off of your life. We will do that, because that's where it started. We will break that initial contact, but after that, it's all about discipleship. It's about renewing your mind to the Word of God.

Prayer always works, and it's always good, because we're to make our requests known unto God in everything. We're always to be praying about everything, but at the same time, prayer is not the answer to everything. We always pray about situations, but the idea is that prayer alone, in and of itself, is not always the answer. There are things you must do to change your situation.

Depression is fear, so essentially, we just cast out that spirit of fear. We break that thing's power and authority over your life. Because you are a Christian, it shouldn't have the power or authority over your life anyway, but you can give it that influence into your life by thinking on the suggestions that it gives you.

Let's go into the Word and get some Scriptures.

Psalms 38:1-6,

> 1 A Psalm of David, to bring to remembrance. O LORD, rebuke me not in thy wrath: neither chasten me in thy hot displeasure.
>
> 2 For thine arrows stick fast in me, and thy hand presseth me sore.
>
> 3 *There is* no soundness in my flesh because of thine anger; neither *is there any* rest in my bones because of my sin.
>
> 4 For mine iniquities are gone over mine head: as an heavy burden they are too heavy for me.
>
> 5 My wounds stink *and* are corrupt because of my foolishness.
>
> 6 I am troubled; I am bowed down greatly; I go mourning all the day long.

"I am troubled; I am bowed down greatly; I go mourning all the day long." Over and over, David says this. He kept saying, "I'm down. I'm depressed." He started talking about it and put it into a Psalm. David was going through a depression because of what he was going through in his life, but he was dwelling upon all of the negative aspects.

How To Beat Depression

1 Kings chapter 19,

> 1 And Ahab told Jezebel all that Elijah had done, and withal how he had slain all the prophets with the sword.
>
> 2 Then Jezebel sent a messenger unto Elijah, saying, So let the gods do *to me,* and more also, if I make not thy life as the life of one of them by to morrow about this time.

In other words, Jezebel was saying to Elijah, "Let the gods do all of these things to me if I don't kill you by tomorrow at this time."

> 3 And when he saw *that,* he arose, and went for his life, and came to Beersheba, which *belongeth* to Judah, and left his servant there.

Elijah had just killed hundreds of prophets of Baal, and here, one woman said, "I'm going to kill you by this time tomorrow," and he got up and ran for his life. Again, he had to think that what she was saying was going to come to pass, so he ran out of fear. "And he came to Beersheba, which belongs to Judah, and he left his servant there."

Starting with verse 4, it tells about Elijah's journey and what all he went through.

In verse 14 He was saying to God,

> 14 And he said, I have been very jealous for the Lord God of hosts: because the children of Israel have forsaken thy covenant, thrown down thine altars, and slain thy

prophets with the sword; and I, even I only, am left; and they seek my life, to take it away.

Elijah said, "Lord I'm the only one left, and they seek my life, to take it away." When he told God that he was the only one, God spoke to him.

In verse 18 God told Elijah,

> 18 Yet I have left me seven thousand in Israel, all the knees which have not bowed unto Baal, and every mouth which hath not kissed him.

God was saying, "You're not the only one. I have 7,000 others. I've got more hidden. You're not the only one going through this thing."

Here's the thing to remember: no matter what you're going through, somebody else has gone through it. What I mean is that they have gone through it; they didn't just suffer it. They have gone through it and beaten it. They've come out on the other side of it.

Essentially, what this comes down to is simply to stop thinking about what you've been thinking about. Decide to change your mind. If you don't decide to change your thoughts and to change what you're focusing on, there isn't a person in the world who can help you. You have to make the decision to quit thinking on the things that are bad and the things that are negative.

I'm not saying to ignore the negative things or act as if they don't exist. You have to deal with them. To deal with them means that you take care of them, and then you set them aside.

It's not that you're ignoring them; you just have to deal with them. You deal with them according to the Word and according to the Spirit of God.

Remember: the reason we're talking about this is because so many people in America and around the world suffer depression, and it is not God's will. Depression is never God's will. He wants you to have the joy of the Lord within you. Depression usually comes because you are dwelling on things that are outside of your control. The joy of the Lord is within you, and no matter what goes on around you, you have that joy. When you have that joy, you don't get depressed.

When I was with Dr. Sumrall, I remember him saying, "Well, there're three things that bring ministries down. It's the gold, the glory, and the girls. Stay away from the gold; don't get enamored with the finances. Stay away from the glory; Give God credit for everything that He does. Stay away from the girls; don't be messing around with the women." He said those were the three things that would cause trouble.

He also said, "As a minister, the thing you're going to fight the most, even above the gold, the glory, and the girls, is depression." He said, "Ministers fight against depression more than any other one thing. That's because they want to advance the Gospel. They know the vision. They know the call that God has on their life, and they know where they should be going with it. Many times things don't seem to be moving as fast as they know they should, and because of that, they think, 'Well, if it was just me, I could make these things happen, but I have to depend on this person or that person,' or 'I have to deal with this, or wait for that.' There are circumstances that we would say are outside of our control, and because of that, we can't control other people's will, so we get depressed." He warned, "Always stay on guard against depression."

Usually, when depression hits, it is right after a victory. Usually you will go through some great victory, and all of a sudden, the enemy comes in to hit something. He will hit in some other area and cause a setback. You'll take a nosedive into depression, which makes no sense logically. You ought to be able to look at the previous victory and go right on through the depression.

However, depression doesn't have to make sense. It is fear and worry about future things, not about reality.

1 Samuel chapter 30,

> 1 And it came to pass, when David and his men were come to Ziklag on the third day, that the Amalekites had invaded the south, and Ziklag, and smitten Ziklag, and burned it with fire;
>
> 2 And had taken the women captives, that *were* therein: they slew not any, either great or small, but carried *them* away, and went on their way.

Now get this picture: David went out to fight a battle, and when he got back, the Amalekites had attacked his home base and burned the city. It says that they had taken the women and children captive that were there, but they didn't kill them. They didn't come home and find their wives and children dead; they were all just gone. They were taken captive, which is sometimes harder than finding someone dead.

> 3 So David and his men came to the city, and, behold, *it was* burned with fire; and their wives, and their sons, and their daughters, were taken captives.
>
> 4 Then David and the people that *were* with him lifted up their voice and wept, until they had no more power to weep.

That is depression. They got into depression because they came home and had this overwhelming thing in front of them. All of them, including David himself, began to weep to the point where they could not cry anymore.

> 5 And David's two wives were taken captives, Ahinoam the Jezreelitess, and Abigail the wife of Nabal the Carmelite.
>
> 6 And David was greatly distressed; for the people spake of stoning him, because the soul of all the people was grieved, every man for his sons and for his daughters: but David encouraged himself in the LORD his God.

"And David was greatly distressed." It was depression. "David was greatly distressed for the people spoke of stoning him." Do you hear that? David was leading an army. They went off, they fought, they won, and they did good things. They came back, and their village was burned, their wives were taken captive, and their kids were gone. Everything was taken. They cried and cried until they couldn't cry anymore. Then, David heard his own men talking about stoning him, because he was the one whose fault it was. Why? That's because he was the one who led them into a battle. He had them to go off somewhere else and leave their families unprotected.

Obviously they couldn't hit the Amalekites, so instead they decided to strike out at David. That's something he should have watched for, because it says, "Because the soul of all the people was grieved, every man for his sons and for his daughters."

Now, watch what it says that David did: "David encouraged himself in the LORD, his God." That's the key. Even though they were all discouraged, they were all depressed, and they were all grieving, David shook himself out of that depression. It says that even though they were talking about stoning him because they were grieved over losing their sons and their daughters, David encouraged himself. That was because he had no one else to encourage him. Most of the time, you're going to have to be your own encourager. You're going to have to decide to encourage yourself, because you know all of the things that will encourage you the most.

Notice how he did it: "He encouraged himself in the Lord, his God." Whether you're sitting by yourself, or whether you're in a group, you can be in depression. In a group, people might not even know that you're in depression. Why? That's because you've learned how to act around people. You have to be able to learn, even if you're in depression, how to encourage yourself in the Lord. When every voice you hear is negative and is telling you to quit and give up, you have to decide to encourage yourself in the Lord. It's just you and God.

When you stand before God, you're going to stand there alone. You're going to stand there and answer for everything you've done. You're going to get the good deeds that the Bible says you're going to get rewarded for while you are standing by yourself. You're not going to be able to stand there and say,

"Well, she wouldn't let me, or he wouldn't let me do this. I wanted to support orphans, but he wouldn't let me write a tithe check, or he wouldn't let me write a check for offering." No, you are going to answer to God for yourself. You have to decide for yourself what you're going to do.

You have to learn to encourage yourself in the Lord, because there won't always be people around to encourage you. You have to learn to be able to talk to yourself. This may sound silly, but it has been said that people who talk to themselves are crazy, but that's only when they start answering themselves. No, I am just kidding. It really is a sign of good mental health when you talk to yourself and when you think in conversation with yourself.

I talk to myself constantly. I preach to myself. Every sermon I've ever preached, I have preached to myself probably 30, 40, 50 times before anybody else ever heard it. Why? It's the Word of God, and as I preach it to myself, I get fed.

Many times, I can't find anyone to listen to who feeds me, so I'll preach to myself. I preach right out of the Word of God. A lot of times, I'll just take the Word of God, and read it, and as I read it, then I will talk to myself and explain it to myself and say, "This is what's going on," and as I do that, the revelation that comes out is amazing! Learn to encourage yourself in the Lord.

I have already said that if you don't change the way you think, then you're not going to stay out of depression. We can break that thing off of you, but we want to show you some details of how it's done.

Isaiah 26:3,

> 3 Thou wilt keep *him* in perfect peace, *whose* mind *is* stayed *on thee:* because he trusteth in thee.

I can't whitewash this. I can't water it down. I just have to tell you the exact truth of the Word of God. The Bible says, point blank, no *if*s, *and*s, or *but*s, "God will keep you in perfect peace if you keep your mind stayed on Him," so if your mind is not in perfect peace, and if you are not in perfect peace, your mind is not stayed on Him. It's that simple.

I've had people come to me and say, "Well, I meditate on the Lord, and my mind is on Him, but I just worry…" No. If you're worried, and if this is a continuing thing, your mind is not stayed on Him. That's just a fact. "No, my mind is stayed on Him." No. Either you're lying or God's lying, therefore, you're lying. It's that simple. God said that He will keep you in perfect peace if you will keep your mind on Him.

This isn't easy. It's simple, but it's not easy. The answer is very simple, keep your mind stayed on Him. The answer's not easy, because all of the things going on in the world are geared to get your mind off of Him. All the cares of the world, all the cares of the deceitfulness of riches, and all of these other things are geared to swarm you and to overwhelm you to the place where your mind is stayed on the things around you, rather than stayed on Him.

If you keep your mind stayed on Him, you will stay in a state of perfect peace. If you're not in a state of perfect peace, then your mind is not stayed upon Him. You may be thinking about Him 99.5% of the time, but the other 1/2 of 1% you're worried, thinking about the things that are going on. You think, "Well, we've got this bill. We don't have the money to pay the bill. How are we going to pay the bill?"

I'm not saying that you ignore those things. I'm saying that you have to be able to look to God and say, "Father, You said that You've never seen the righteous forsaken nor his seed begging bread. I can't pay my bills. You said that You are my provider. You said that it is Your pleasure to give me the Kingdom. You said that if I would seek first the Kingdom and Your righteousness then all of these things would be added to me. You said that I wouldn't have to worry about what I am going to eat, or what I am going to wear, or where I'm going to live. You said that you would take care of me, so Father, right now, I roll the cares of these things over to You to take care of. In Jesus' name, I receive two things, right now: the answer to the problem, and the peace that is going to be in my heart. I have that peace, because You are my peace. Amen."

As you start to do that, then God will start to supernaturally manifest the answers to the problems and situations you've got going on, but you have to keep your mind stayed on Him.

Again, I cannot say this enough: it is not an easy thing. You have to make the decision to decide to keep your mind on Him.

There are going to be people around you who are constantly telling you, "This isn't going to work," or "That isn't going work." You have to decide and say, "I hear you, but I'm not listening to you. The Bible says that the voice of another I will not hear. I'm listening to God. His voice says that He will keep me in perfect peace. His voice says that He is my provider, and that I am blessed with every spiritual blessing in heavenly places. Therefore I hear what you are saying, but I choose not to agree with you. I choose to agree with Him." If you do that, your heart will be at peace.

People will look at you, and they'll think you're just in denial and that you're ignoring the problem. They will say that you're just not in reality. No, this is reality. The Spirit realm is reality. The Spirit realm is the real thing, and if you stick with God, and stay on His Word, then the spirit realm will become the natural realm to you. Your natural realm will change, and the circumstances will change.

You're not the one exception in the entire universe for whom God's Word won't work. Do you understand that? It is the height of arrogance to think that you're in a situation where God can't help you.

You cannot dig a hole so deep that God can't get you out of it. No matter what problem you're in, God is bigger than that problem. He can't help you if you don't look to Him. He can't help you if your mind is not stayed upon Him. You have to trust Him, look to Him, and recognize the situations going on around you. You have to deal with them through prayer. Decide to think on the things you're supposed to think on.

Let's look at Philippians 4:8 again to see what those are. It says,

> 8 Finally, brethren, whatsoever things are true, whatsoever things *are* honest, whatsoever things *are* just, whatsoever things *are* pure, whatsoever things *are* lovely, whatsoever things *are* of good report; if *there be*

any virtue, and if *there be* any praise, think on these things.

You are to think on things that are true, not things of fear. That is a command. You do not have the right to think on those other things.

I have no tolerance for people who just want to sit around and talk about the problem. If you want to talk about solutions, fine. However, if you want to talk about problems, I will leave the room, because my mind is going to be on things that are good, pure, holy, and of good report, and all of the things mentioned in this verse. I am going to think on those things.

My mind is going to be stayed on God. In Proverbs 10:19 it tells us,

> 19 In the multitude of words there wanteth not sin: but he that refraineth his lips *is* wise.

That's because people talk. When they first start talking, they may talk for about five minutes in faith giving praise to God and testimonies and then, as soon as they run out of things to say, unfortunately, they don't stop talking. They continue talking when they run out of things to say and, because of that, they get over into sin. They get into fear, and they get into problems. They start worrying about future problems. They start telling you about everything, "Did you hear about so and so? Oh, they're having this thing." Okay, that's gossip.

If that is you, you need to stop it. You don't need to talk about it. If you've got a situation with someone, you pray for them. You don't talk about them to other people.

If you're in a leadership situation, then you need to know the things that are going on. You need to know the circumstances so that you can deal with them and fix them, not just to be passing on negative information. Understand, if there's a problem that needs to be dealt with, you have to decide how to deal with it, but don't gossip.

When someone calls me, it has to be about something important. Don't talk about unnecessary things and go on and on. I don't want to talk on the phone. I have prayer requests. I have things going on. I have people to pray for. I do not need conversation. I don't need anyone calling and talking to me for 45 minutes about nothing. If they do, then the next time they call, I'm not going to answer the call. Why? I don't have time to waste for just talk, especially if it is just to go on and on. If someone has something to say, they need to make a complete sentence, and say it. They can say it, get it out, we'll talk about it, and move on.

My time is valuable. What I mean by that is that I don't have a lot of extra time. If I'm not praying for people, I am studying. I want to be studying and reading the Word of God. I want to spend my time in fellowship with God, not just talking about what is going on that day. Very honestly, most people's lives are not interesting enough to spend a lot of time talking about them.

If you're going to talk about your life, make it interesting. That means that you should go and do something interesting, and then talk about it. I am just being blunt, but I am just letting you know that I'm not going to just talk on the phone for hours and say nothing. I have too many other people that need help.

How To Beat Depression

Most people end up in depression, because they rehearse. Have you ever noticed that when you start talking with a person, they'll tell you a horrible story, and you think, "Okay, let's get to the point where I can tell you the answer and where I can help you fix it."

By the way, men usually want to fix things, and women just want to talk about things. That's just generally the way women and men are; they're just different. When a woman tells a man a problem, the man is thinking, "Okay, I'm trying to figure out how to fix this," whereas women are just thinking, "I just want you to be quiet and listen." That's the difference in the way men and women think.

Someone will tell you a story and then, while you're sitting there, someone else will walk into the room, and they will rehearse the same story to the next person. If you're there with that person for 30 minutes, you will hear that same story 10 times. It is told to everybody that walks in and is constantly being rehearsed. Quit! In the words of Bob Newhart, "Stop it! Just stop it!" You don't have to rehearse every problem. You don't have to tell everybody, every problem. Let's get focused on the things that are good and of pure report. Keep your mind steady.

Again, in 2 Timothy 1:7 we read,

> 7 For God hath not given us the spirit of fear; but of power, and of love, and of a sound mind.

Sound mind! That means that you have clarity of thought. You think in terms of sound doctrine. You think accurately. You're not going to think with a sound mind if you're going to constantly rehearse problems. You have to constantly rehearse the solution, which is the Word of God. Think on the Word of God. Preach the Word of God. Speak the Word of God.

You're going to have to get obsessed, and you're going to have to get to the place where nobody wants to tell you unnecessary things. They may tell you a problem so that you can pray about it or deal with it, but don't get involved to the point where they are just constantly rehearsing and rehashing these things.

Hebrews 2:13-15,

> 13 And again, I will put my trust in him. And again, Behold I and the children which God hath given me.
>
> 14 Forasmuch then as the children are partakers of flesh and blood, he also himself likewise took part of the same; that through death he might destroy him that had the power of death, that is, the devil;
>
> 15 And deliver them who through fear of death were all their lifetime subject to bondage.

Do you hear that? "Through fear of death, they were all their lifetime subject to bondage." You've got to destroy the fear of death. If you're going to have fear of death, you will always be subject to bondage. The enemy will always be able to put you in bondage through fear of death. If you allow him to do that, the fear of death will spread out into every other area of your life.

Go to Hebrews chapter 13. I hope this is helping you as far as trying to understand depression. Depression is never God's will, and we can break the spirit of fear over you, but the only way for you to get out of it is for you to change your thinking. Think on things that are good, and pure, and holy, and of good report. Put your mind on God, and keep your mind on Him, and you'll stay in peace. It's very simple.

Hebrews 13:5-6,

> 5 *Let your* conversation *be* without covetousness; *and be* content with such things as ye have: for he hath said, I will never leave thee, nor forsake thee.

If you do this, it will stop a lot of depression. A lot of depression is caused by people watching depressing television programs or television commercials that tell them that they should have much more than they have. They are never satisfied, because they're always thinking, "Well, I need this, or I should have that, or I should have this other thing." No. Be content with what you have. It says, "For He hath said, 'I will never leave thee, nor forsake thee.'"

> 6 So that we may boldly say, The Lord *is* my helper, and I will not fear what man shall do unto me.

Because you know that He will never leave you nor forsake you, you can boldly say, "The Lord is my helper, and I will not fear what man shall do unto me." To be able to say that boldly means to say it with conviction, "I will not fear! The Lord is my helper! I will not fear what man shall do to me!" You have to say it with a strong voice, with boldness.

Go with me to 1 John 4:15-18,

> 15 Whosoever shall confess that Jesus is the Son of God, God dwelleth in him, and he in God.

> 16 And we have known and believed the love that God hath to us. God is love; and he that dwelleth in love dwelleth in God, and God in him.
>
> 17 Herein is our love made perfect, that we may have boldness in the day of judgment: because as he is, so are we in this world.

"Herein," you dwelling in Him, and Him dwelling in you, "is our love made perfect, that we may have boldness in the Day of Judgment, because as He is, so are we in this world."

> 18 There is no fear in love; but perfect love casteth out fear: because fear hath torment. He that feareth is not made perfect in love.

"Fear has torment." If you stay in the love of God, you won't have torment; you won't have fear, because fear brings torment. Torment is depression. It is constant fear. It is constant worrying, and when you are in fear, and torment, and in depression, you are not dwelling in the love of God. Your mind is not on Him, and you won't have peace. It's that simple.

Let us pray:

"Right now, in the name of Jesus, if you are in depression, fear, I break your power! You have no right here, and you will go now, in the name of Jesus! I set you free! Right now, those who are depressed, I command you, 'Be free.') Right now, may the peace of God be upon you.

"Right now, you repent. Change your mind. Right now, turn your mind around, and decide today, 'I will keep my mind stayed upon God. I will think on things that are pure, and holy, and of good report. I will think on things that are right. I will do the right thing. I will choose to think upon good things. I will choose to think upon the Word of God. I will encourage myself in the Lord.' You make that decision.

"Right now, in the name of Jesus, I'm commanding you to be free. That spirit of fear, that spirit of torment, has to go now, in Jesus' name. Be free!

"Right now, decide; do not dwell upon, meditate upon, or think about the negative, and the things that can bring fear. Instead, dwell upon and meditate upon the Word of God and the fact that He is your Provider. He is your Everything. He will take care of you. He's your Healer. If you say, 'Well, I'm depressed because I'm sick,' He will heal you. He's Jehovah Rapha, the Lord that heals.

"By His stripes you are healed! Be free now, in the name of Jesus! Amen. Amen."

FREEDOM FROM DEPRESSION

REPLACING FEAR WITH FAITH

We are talking about depression. Therefore, we are talking about fear. We're talking about anxiety and all of the things that are coming upon the world with an ever-increasing rate.

In looking at anxiety and depression, it's not just enough to talk about it; it's not enough to tell you details and statistics. We have to get you free of it. We can get you free, but then you have to stay free. We have to teach you how to stay free. That's discipleship. Deliverance gets you free. Discipleship is learning how to keep yourself free. Then you can go out and get other people free, so it's important.

You have to make that decision to stay free. No one can make it for you. As I said, we can set you free, but if you don't make that decision to stay free, you will go right back into bondage again.

Fear is an enemy. We can talk about depression, anxiety, or any of those things, but what we're really talking about is fear. The Bible tells us that we have not been given a spirit of fear, but we have been given a spirit of power, a spirit of love, and a spirit of a sound mind.

Paul was writing to his young disciple Timothy in 2 Timothy chapter 1:

> 5 When I call to remembrance the unfeigned faith that is in thee, which dwelt first in thy grandmother Lois, and

thy mother Eunice; and I am persuaded that in thee also.

"When I call to remembrance the unfeigned faith that is in you…" Everybody should have a person that they know that they can call, get in touch with, and talk to who has that "unfeigned faith." They know that whenever they see that person, the person is going to look at them and say, "I know what you've got! I know what you're capable of! I know what's in you! You can do this! You will overcome! You are bigger than this thing, because God is in you, and God is bigger than this thing!" Every person needs to have a person like that in their life. You just need to find somebody like that. After you find that somebody, get around them, and stay around them as much as you can.

Paul says, "When I call to remembrance the unfeigned faith that is in you, which dwelt first in your grandmother Lois, and your mother Eunice; and I am persuaded that in you, also." He was telling Timothy, "I'm convinced. I know what's in you."

> 6 Wherefore I put thee in remembrance that thou stir up the gift of God, which is in thee by the putting on of my hands.

Paul was saying, "I put my hands on you. I know what's in you, but you've got to stir it up. You can't just say, 'Well, God stir me up. God give me revival. God wake me up.'" He said, "No, you stir up the gift that is in you. You do it!" This was a command.

In verse 7 it says,

> 7 For God hath not given us the spirit of fear; but of power, and of love, and of a sound mind.

Do you hear that? You have a spirit of power, you have a spirit of love, and you have a spirit of a sound mind. These are not "ifs, ands, or buts." You don't have a spirit of fear. God has not given you a spirit of fear.

A spirit of fear can attack you, and if you let it sit on your shoulder, and talk in your ear, and you don't rebuke that thing, then you're going to go back into even deeper bondage than you were in before. Get it off of you, or you're going to stay in bondage.

If that spirit of fear is trying to get on you, and trying to tell you things, you have to make a decision. You need to stop, right then, and say, "Oh, no you don't! You're not from God."

There will be times when the enemy will talk to you through people. You need to be able to look at them and say, "I hear you, but I'm not going to listen to you. If you're going to continue to talk this way, we are not going to continue to fellowship. You need to talk about the Word of God. You need to talk about what God can do in and through you, not what the devil can do." You need to let those people know that, and you need to find people that will tell you what God can do through you.

If a spirit of fear is on you, if you have depression, or if you have anxiety, you need to know that it is not from God. You have to say, "You're not from God." You have to decide that the voice whispering in your ear is not from God. You say, "God has not given me a spirit of fear, but of power. I have the spirit of power. I have the spirit of love."

"Well, I don't feel like I love people." It doesn't matter; you have the spirit of love. You've got to stir up the gift that's in you. Sometimes you have to stir up love, and sometimes you have to stir up power. You have a spirit of a sound mind. To have a sound mind, you've got to think on sound doctrine. You've got to think on sound things. You can't think on stupid, wrong things, and have a sound mind.

If you don't have a sound mind, that is not God's fault. He has given you a spirit of a sound mind, but you have to decide to be able to walk in these things and think on these things.

He's told you how to have a sound mind.

> 1. Keep your mind stayed upon God, and He'll keep you in perfect peace.
>
> 2. Think on things that are good, pure, holy, and of good report.

He said, "Think on these things." He didn't say to think on the 6 o'clock news. He said, "Think on good things." He says, "For God hath not given us the spirit of fear; but of power, and of love, and of a sound mind."

If you're going through depression, you may be having problems, or maybe something just stays with you, and you're afraid of that. A wife might think, "Well, I'm afraid my husband's going to leave me for somebody else. I'm afraid he's going to do this." A husband may think, "Well, I'm afraid my wife is running around on me, or I'm afraid that something else is going on."

If you don't know that's going on, then that's a spirit of fear, and you need to stop that thing. If you are a husband, you need to start saying out loud, "I love my wife. She loves me. She wouldn't cheat on me. I'm not going to cheat on her."

If you're a wife, you need to say the same thing about your husband. You say, "Well, he's got a history of it." So what! We've all got histories of something. Everybody's got a history of something, but at some point you have to say, "I choose to trust. I choose to have faith in him. If nothing else, I choose to have faith in God in him so that I will be able to say, 'I love my husband. He loves me. We're in this thing together; we're going to be together the rest of our lives.'"

You need to start killing those voices of fear and anxiety to where you're not dwelling on those things. You need to dwell on the things that are right and good. Dwell on the Scriptures.

In 2 Timothy 1:13-14 Paul said,

> 13 Hold fast the form of sound words, which thou hast heard of me, in faith and love which is in Christ Jesus.
>
> 14 That good thing which was committed unto thee keep by the Holy Ghost which dwelleth in us.

Paul was trying to tell Timothy, his young disciple, "Stick with the Word. Stick with me. Stay strong. Stir up the gift that is in you."

Go with me to Psalms 78:1-4,

> 1 Give ear, O my people, *to* my law: incline your ears to the words of my mouth.
>
> 2 I will open my mouth in a parable: I will utter dark sayings of old:
>
> 3 Which we have heard and known, and our fathers have told us.
>
> 4 We will not hide *them* from their children, shewing to the generation to come the praises of the LORD, and his strength, and his wonderful works that he hath done.

Notice: "We will not hide them from their children, showing to the generation to come the praises of the Lord." If you have children, you need to be telling your children what you know that God has done, whether they are Bible stories or whether they are testimonies out of your own life. You really need to have a mixture of both.

You need to start telling your children, at an early age, what God has done. "This is what God did for the Israelites. This is what God did for our family. This is what God has done through us." You should have praises to give to God, and they should be shared with your children.

One of the reasons why so many children are not following God as they grow up today is because they haven't heard anything. They just go to church, and most of the time all they hear is condemnation.

Psalms 78:5-6,

> 5 For he established a testimony in Jacob, and appointed a law in Israel, which he commanded our fathers, that they should make them known to their children:

Notice he commanded the fathers. He didn't say, "Don't worry fathers; it's My responsibility as God to make sure your kids hear the Law." No. He said, "Fathers, it is your responsibility to make sure that your children know the Word of God."

> 6 That the generation to come might know *them, even* the children *which* should be born; *who* should arise and declare *them* to their children:

In other words, every generation should be raised up; fathers should preach it to their children. When those children grow up and become fathers, they are to preach it to their children. This continues on. Your grandchildren and great-grandchildren should know the things that God has done for you in your life, so write those things down.

There used to be a book called "Book of Yasher" where they wrote down the testimonies. It was almost like a 'National Archives for Israel.' They told about all of the good things that God had done for them. You need a "Book of Yasher." You need to write your own book of testimonies.

Go all the way back, talk about how your great-grandmother got saved, if they were saved. Talk about their experiences and what God did for them. Go and talk to some of your relatives and get testimonies from your family. Write these things down and then share them with your kids, and share them with your grandkids. Sit around with them on your knee, and tell them the great things that God has done.

When you do this, you're doing two things.

Number one: your mind is being stayed on God, and He will keep you in perfect peace. Even while you're sharing that, you're getting stronger, and you are creating neuro pathways in your own mind of how to think correctly.

Number two: by doing that, you're also training your children how to think accurately and how to think in line with praising God. You will give them a sound mind, because you're teaching them how to keep their minds stayed on God, therefore, He will also keep them in perfect peace.

This is what fathers are supposed to do with their children. Notice that it doesn't say mothers, although mothers are doing this. I know that in today's world it means both, but honestly, it tells the fathers that they should be sitting down with their children. Why? That's because the father is usually the authority figure, and if he's telling his children that it is important, then most of the time they will take it as important.

Psalms 78:6, 7,

> 6 That the generation to come might know *them, even* the children *which* should be born; *who* should arise and declare *them* to their children:
>
> 7 That they might set their hope in God, and not forget the works of God, but keep his commandments:

"That they might set their hope in God…" Do you hear that? The reason they're going to set their hope in God is because they hear the testimonies of the great things that God has done for them. While you're telling your children what God has done for you in your life, what He's done for the Israelites through the Bible stories, and giving them different testimonies, you're also showing them that they can set their hope in God. You're giving them a basis for faith.

"Well, I would like to do that, but I just don't have time. I'm at work from early in the morning before they get up, and by the time I get home, they're already in bed." Then change jobs! "Well, I can't, because I have to make enough money for this house." Get a smaller house. Get a cheaper house. Do something else. What's important is what is eternal, not the temporal things. It's the eternal things that are important.

We want our children to set their hope in God, and not forget the works of God, but keep his commandments.

1 John 2:3,

> 3 And hereby we do know that we know him, if we keep his commandments.

Years ago, starting in the 40s and into the 50s, we started seeing men of God like A. A. Allen, Jack Coe, and various other people on television every week. First they would preach for 10 or 15 minutes and then they would do a healing service.

They would show people getting healed, getting out of wheelchairs, and giving praise to God. Their testimonies were being made known throughout the United States through television every week.

Then that stopped, and people quit having those kinds of meetings, for the most part. People stopped seeing all of that, and they started watching other television programs. What ended up happening is that the kids ended up watching stupid things that took faith out of them, rather than watching things like healing on television that put faith in them. Because of that, it all eventually died out. They weren't able to set their hope in God, because they didn't hear the testimonies and things of God.

In many of the Christian churches today, you hear people say, "Healing passed away with the Apostles," or "Oh, that's not real," or "Those tongues are of the devil." You have all of these people saying all these contrary things.

Your children are not going to set their faith in God when they have been told that everything in the Bible has passed away. They're not going to set their faith in God whenever they think God won't help them like He did the Israelites.

You have to bring the children's attention back to God. You say, "God will help you. He helped us. He helped our grandparents. He'll help you, just like He did the Israelites. He'll help you just like He helps anybody else."

Let's go back and start with verse 7 of Psalms 78,

> 7 That they might set their hope in God, and not forget the works of God, but keep his commandments:

> 8 And might not be as their fathers, a stubborn and rebellious generation; a generation *that* set not their heart aright, and whose spirit was not stedfast with God.

In other words, if you don't do this, here's what's going to happen: they're not going to set their hearts on God. They're not going to be steadfast with God, and they'll fall away.

> 9 The children of Ephraim, *being* armed, *and* carrying bows, turned back in the day of battle.

They didn't have faith that God would provide for them and that God would give them the victory. They didn't have faith that He would take care of them, so whenever they came up against a bigger army, they turned and ran, rather than being like the valiant warriors of David, who would charge into them, in which case a much smaller force beat a bigger force.

> 10 They kept not the covenant of God, and refused to walk in his law;
>
> 11 And forgat his works, and his wonders that he had shewed them.
>
> 12 Marvellous things did he in the sight of their fathers, in the land of Egypt, *in* the field of Zoan.
>
> 13 He divided the sea, and caused them to pass through; and he made the waters to stand as an heap.

"He divided the sea." In verse 14, he starts to talk about some of the great things that they had seen.

Psalms 78:14,

> 14 In the daytime also he led them with a cloud, and all the night with a light of fire.

He was rehearsing all of these things that God had done.

Psalms 78:15-19,

> 15 He clave the rocks in the wilderness, and gave *them* drink as *out of* the great depths.
>
> 16 He brought streams also out of the rock, and caused waters to run down like rivers.
>
> 17 And they sinned yet more against him by provoking the most High in the wilderness.
>
> 18 And they tempted God in their heart by asking meat for their lust.
>
> 19 Yea, they spake against God; they said, Can God furnish a table in the wilderness?

Do you hear that? It says, "They spoke against God by saying, 'Can God do this?'" When you question God and ask if He can do something, you are speaking against God.

Psalms 78:20,

> 20 Behold, he smote the rock that the waters gushed out, and the streams overflowed; can he give bread also? Can he provide flesh for his people?

Again, they were asking, "Can He do this? Is He big enough?" Again, they were speaking against God saying, "Can He provide flesh for His people?"

Psalms 78:21-26,

> 21 Therefore the LORD heard *this,* and was wroth: so a fire was kindled against Jacob, and anger also came up against Israel;
>
> 22 Because they believed not in God, and trusted not in his salvation:
>
> 23 Though he had commanded the clouds from above, and opened the doors of heaven,
>
> 24 And had rained down manna upon them to eat, and had given them of the corn of heaven.
>
> 25 Man did eat angels' food: he sent them meat to the full.
>
> 26 He caused an east wind to blow in the heaven: and by his power he brought in the south wind.

People say, "I know what God did in the Bible, but honestly, can He help me pay my mortgage?" or "Honestly, do you think God's big enough to cure me? Come on! This is cancer we're talking about." When people do this, they are talking against God.

We have to rest in His salvation, but the first thing we have to do is get rid of the fear of death. If you get rid of the fear of death, you won't be in bondage to fear anymore, because fear has torment. You will start to live in the love of God. When you live in the love of God, you understand that God will take care of you. He loves you. He will take care of you no matter what. I don't care what comes upon this earth; He will take care of you if your faith is in Him.

If you want to be free, don't spend all of your time watching garbage and listening to garbage. This includes things on television, in movies, or anything else that is anti-God. It also means not to listen to preaching that says God only helps you if you send in money, or God will only do this if you do something else. No.

You have to get your faith in God, now. You're not going to go watch all of this garbage and then whenever something happens, all of a sudden, you're going to jump up and think you have faith in God. You're not! You have to develop faith in God, now. You have to know that God is your God.

One of the saddest stories that I ever heard happened back in 1937. John Lake passed away in 1935. He had a son named Roderick who was born in 1920. When John Lake passed away, Roderick was 15 years old. In 1937, when Roderick was 17, he lay dying in his bed. He told the people around him, "I know that if my father were here, I wouldn't have to die."

That's the saddest thing. John Lake had almost a quarter of a million testimonies of confirmed and documented healings. There were healings of every kind of disease, and those were just here in the United States. That was from five years in Spokane and five years in Portland. That does not even include the five years he had in South Africa, where there were hundreds of thousands of healings and amazing miracles.

Roderick was raised up in the midst of all of these things, and he saw some of these things going on. He had heard about some of the things that happened with his Dad, and here he was, lying on his deathbed, saying, "If only my Dad were here." He never should have had to say, "If my Dad were here." He should have been able to say, "The God that heard my Dad's prayers is my God also, and He will hear my prayers." He should've been able to say, "I've heard the things that God did for my Dad, and I know He will do this for me," but he didn't.

The faith that was in John Lake's heart did not transfer over to his family. It's a sad thing that his 17-year-old son had to die with those words on his lips. That is wrong. It's just not right.

We, as a people of God, have a right to have a testimony. We have a right to the things of God. We have a right to be able to stand and boldly say, "I know my God is with me. I don't care what man can do. I don't care what happens or what's going on around me. I don't care what the economy does. My God is with me, and I will come through this. I will overcome it!"

When the Depression hit in 1929, John Lake was in Spokane. He had a brand new Ford car, and some of his family asked, "What are we going to do? Are we going to cut back because of the depression? Are we going to sell the car? Are we going to cut back on some things?"

John Lake said, "No! We won't cut back. We go forward! We get stronger!" He said, "The people are looking to us. If we show fear, or if we show doubt, it will relate to the people, and it will bleed over into them. We have to show the people that we trust God." He said, "We don't cut back; we go forward. We get bigger. We do more; we have to advance."

If you're going to base everything you do on the economy of the world and this world's system, it is your god. You have to decide that God is your God. He will take care of you, regardless of the economy and regardless of the system.

You say, "I thought we were going to talk about anxiety and depression?" What do you think is bringing on most of the anxiety and depression in the world today? It's the economy. The idea is that people are worried, and they are fearful that they're going to lose their homes, or they're going to lose their cars, or they're going to lose this thing or that thing.

People are afraid of losing their jobs. I'm here to tell you that if you lose your job, God can get you a better one. Have faith in Him. In the meantime, while you're looking for one, God will provide for you. He will take care of you. Move forward; advance.

Don't operate out of fear. Don't even pray out of fear. One of the reasons we don't have answered prayers, sometimes, is because people pray out of fear. God doesn't answer prayers that are prayed out of fear. He answers prayers that are prayed in faith. You have to have faith in Him. Don't pray prayers out of fear.

Decide to move forward. Decide to go after the things of God. Decide that God is your God! He is your God. He will take care of you. Have faith in God. This is not just talk; you've got to get started now. You need it before the storm arises.

We saw it with Jesus, and we saw it with Peter. They were both in the same storm in the same boat. The disciples were there with Jesus, who was sleeping in the back of the boat, while the storm was going on. All of the disciples went to Jesus and said, "Master, don't you care? We're going to die." He said, "You faithless bunch!" He got up, and He rebuked the wind and the sea. The wind and the sea calmed down, and they were amazed at the fact that the wind and sea obeyed Him.

Jesus was amazed at the fact that they didn't get up and talk to the wind and the sea saying, "Wind and sea, calm down! The Son of the living God is in the back of this boat, and He told us to go to the other side. He didn't tell us to come out to the middle and drown in a storm. Storm, stop! Sea, calm down! Have peace now!"

Instead, they were full of fear. The difference is that they had not developed faith in God and knowing that He was with them. They had faith in the fact that Jesus was there, but even then they were like, "Don't You care? Aren't You going to do something?"

That's no different than what Christians do today. "God, don't You care? Don't You see what I'm going through? God, what's the matter? Don't You even care about me? What's going on? Why is this happening to me?"

If you were to talk to Jesus right now, and you started saying, "Well, don't You even care?" do you know what He's going to say to you? "You faithless bunch! I told you before, 'Have faith. With God all things are possible. To him that believeth, all things are possible.' You get up! You speak to the mountain! You tell it to move!" He's not going to say, "Oh, you poor little thing; that's all right. Stand back behind Me, and let Me handle this for you." No, He's not going to handle it for you. He tells you to handle His business for Him.

Today, there is this New Age type Jesus, when what you need is the Bible Jesus. You need a Jesus who says, "Here you go. Do this in My name. In My name, you cast out devils. In My name, you heal the sick. In My name, you take up serpents. In My name, you lay hands on the sick, and they shall recover." He didn't say to go there and to plead with them to leave in His name. He said, "You have to develop faith in the fact that I'm sending you in My stead. Now, you go and act like Me. You talk like Me."

You don't go and talk like Peter. You don't go and talk like Thomas. You go and talk like Jesus. You start speaking these things, and then you have to step up. That's why we talk about John Lake today. That's why we talk about Smith Wigglesworth today. That's why I talk about Dr. Sumrall today. Why? That's because these men didn't sit back and cower. They stepped up and said, "God is with me and because of that, in the name of Jesus, this is the way it will be."

When everybody was cowering, or when everybody was running, and hiding, and trying to plead with God, "Oh, God, where are You? Why aren't You helping me?" then the Sumralls, and the Lakes, and the Wigglesworths would stand up and say, "Shut your cowardice! Stand up! Be like men. Speak with a strong voice. Speak to the mountain about the power of God."

That's who you are! You are this new creation who was created after the likeness of God Himself. God put Himself in you so that you could speak into these situations. He wants you to decree, and He wants you to declare the situation to rise up and become in accordance with the Word of God. As it says very clearly, "Thy will be done on earth as it is in heaven."

When you see a situation, you ask, "Is that the way it would look in heaven?" No. Then fix it until it does look like it would look in heaven. You start speaking to that thing and say, "You will line up, right now, in the name of Jesus!"

"Well, it's terminal." "Shut up!" "But the doctors say…" "Shut up!" Who cares what the doctors say? Who cares what the reports say? If it's not a report that lines up with the Word of God that says, "By His stripes you are healed," then it's an evil report.

Go back into the Bible and look at when the 12 spies went into the Promised Land. Ten came back saying, "Oh, we can't do it. They're too big. It's awful." Only two, Joshua and Caleb, came back and said, "We are well able. Give us this mountain; we'll take it. Let us go in there, and do this."

It said that the 10 spies brought back an evil report, and because of that evil report, they and their families died in the wilderness. The only 2 of the 12 that actually got to go into the Promised Land were Joshua and Caleb. They're the ones that came back with a good report that lined up with the Word of God. Their report said, "Yes, we can do this."

Notice that when God sent them into the Promised Land, He didn't say, "Go in there, and figure out how to take this land." He didn't say, "Come back, and tell Me if you can take this land."

When Moses sent them in, he said, "You go in, and you spy it out. Come back, and tell us when we can go in to take the land. We're going in, and when we do, we will need to take things with us. Find out if there is food there. Find out if they live in walled cities. Find out if we need to take weapons and battering rams with us."

All Moses said was, "I want information. I'm not trying to find out if we can take them. We're going to take the land. What I want to know is some information (what we would call intel) on how they live. We will need to know when we go into this city whether we are going to have to attack a fortress, or are we just going to be able to run through a village."

He wouldn't ask, "Can we do it?" He said, "I just want details. Make maps. Bring back the info on the areas. Give me statistics; let me know how many people are there. Let me know these things, because we are taking this land. I need to figure out a strategy to do it with." All he needed was information, and then they came back and said, "Oh, we can't do it." He didn't send them in there to find out if they could. He sent them in there for intelligence, for information.

Too many people say, "Oh, we can't do this. We can't. We don't have enough money. We don't have enough this, or we don't have enough that." No! You can do whatever God says you can do. You just need to get busy. Whatever you lack, either God Himself will provide, or He'll send people with whatever you lack. You get started first. You don't wait until you have everything. You get started, and then as you need more, God will give you more.

In the Bible, God hardly ever added to. Almost every time, He said, "No, you're too big, and you're too strong. You've got too much. I'm going to have to send some of you home." Do you remember what He said to Gideon? He said, "If I give you this victory now, with what you've got, you will think it was you who did it. I want to make sure that you know that there was no way you could do it, so I want you to send most of your people home."

When people say they don't have enough money, we say, "Great! You're in a perfect position for God to help you." God may tell you, "If you want to build something for Me, or if you want to do something for Me, take that bank account, and empty it. Don't use it for your project; give it to people who are in need."

You say, "God, we're trying to raise money for this project," and He'll say, "Yes, I know, and if you want that, then give the money that you have raised for it to those who are in need. I don't want you doing it with the money you've raised, because then you'll say that you did it. Instead, give it away, and I will do your project for you."

That's the way God thinks, and if you're going to have faith in Him, that's what you're going to think. When you think that way, then money is no longer a god. Situations are no longer a god. Only God is God, and you'll have faith in God, and you'll move forward.

The key with all of this is that you have to decide what you're supposed to do. The worst situation to be in is to not know what you're supposed to do. It's very simple. If you are a believer, then you're commissioned to preach the Gospel, whether you feel like you can preach or not. You are commissioned to be a witness unto the whole world. As a believer, you are commissioned to heal the sick, raise the dead, and cast out devils.

Sometimes when people come here, they come not knowing if God wants them here. They come here because they want to come here, or they come here because they say that Curry gave a call. Yes, I'm giving a call to everybody, but that doesn't mean everybody's going to come. However, if you come, you make sure that you believe that God wants you here. Don't come just because Curry said, "If you want to come down, come down, and do something."

We invite everybody here. I put this out on the internet to where a potential hearing audience can be up to seven billion people. I don't think seven billion people are going to show up in Dallas next week. If you really believe that God wants you here, then come. The good part about that is that whenever you hit some type of resistance, you're not going to say, "Well, Curry called me." No, you're going to say, "God told me to be here. I'm here, and no devil is going to run me off." You have to have that in you.

We have the church going in Plano, Texas. We are holding Church services on Sundays there. If you want to come, come. We're going to be in the building at 1104 Summit Avenue, Suite 102, Plano, Texas. You can come there from 10 o'clock until noon. We are broadcasting from there on Sundays via the internet.

We're going to raise up a strong church for this area that's going to reach into the whole world. The ministry is already reaching the whole world. We want other believers to come and join with us to help us to rise up in this city to establish the Kingdom of God.

Wherever you are, you can be a member of this church. I don't care if you're in South Africa or if you're in Australia; it doesn't make any difference where you are. If you want to be a member of this church, it's easy. You let us know by writing to us, emailing us, calling us, or by going online. Just say, "I want to be a member of your church."

We'll say, "Okay. Fill out this application." It's a simple form; it just gives us basic information. Then, you'll be a member of our church. If you say, "But I can't come there every Sunday," has nothing to do with it. If you want to be a part of this Body, if you have the vision, and if you want to help push the vision forward, then you can be a part of this church.

You say, "Well, I don't have a home church." Well you need one. Here's one. Join with us. You can watch it by internet, or CD, or DVD, or any other way. We can join together, and we can do something great for God. You say, "Well, we shouldn't be concerned." You should be concerned. You should be doing great things for God.

Psalm 78 was reminding the people of the great things that God had done for them and telling them to pass them on to their children. Now, I am going to say some confessions, and I want you to say them with me. Whether you're reading this or watching it by video, I want you to say them out loud. This is right out of our New Man Seminar. We're going to be looking at "Acknowledging What Is in You in Christ Jesus," and it's in

Section 6 in the manual. If you don't have a manual, you can get it online.

All we did was take the Scriptures that we had studied in the first five sections and put them into statements.

I want you to say them out loud. Repeat them after me, right where you are.

- **I am a new creation.**

Just say, "I am a new creation." Say it like you mean it. Say it with conviction. Convince the devil. You know God knows, and He believes it. Believe it or not, the devil knows that it's true; he's just waiting to see if you believe it's true. You have to convince the devil that you know this and that you believe it. You have to say it forcefully enough to make the devil want to back off of you.

Say it with a strong voice. "I am a new creation!" Don't say it weakly like you doubt it, like you're wondering if it's true. Say it with a strong conviction, "I am a new creation!"

You can say it all kinds of ways. You can say it at least five ways. Put more emphasis when you say the words in bold as follows:

"**I** am a new creation."

"I **am** a new creation."

"I am **a** new creation."

"I am a **new** creation."

"I am a new **creation**."

Do the same thing again with this declaration:

> "**Old** things are passed away."
>
> "Old **things** are passed away."
>
> "Old things **are** passed away."
>
> "Old things are **passed** away."
>
> "Old things are passed **away**."

You just say it over, and over, and over again. Say it out loud. Say it like you believe it.

Here's the next one: **All things in me are new**. Say it out loud. Say it like you mean it. You just keep repeating it. Say it for yourself three, four, or five times. Say it all kinds of ways. Say it with a strong voice. The idea is that you get this in you, because it's in your spirit right now. This is who you are.

You're not trying to make these things real. These are real. What you're trying to do is implant them into your mind. You're renewing your mind. The Bible says to renew your mind to the Word of God. That's what we're doing. It's already a reality, but the reason you're not experiencing a lot of the reality is because you have a filter called your mind.

Your mind filters out a lot of things and goes by the way you think normally. We have to change the way you think; this is done by the renewing of the mind. You renew your mind by saying these things. These are according to what the Word of God says. You say them in a way to where they literally delete the old and replace them with the new. It's almost like the new has to override the old.

Now do this one: **All things in me are of God.**

And now this one: **I am reconciled to God by Jesus Christ.**

"I am reconciled to God by Jesus Christ," means that God and I are together. We're reconciled. We used to be apart, but we aren't any longer. Now we are reconciled, and we are brought back together, in union.

- **God has given me the ministry of reconciliation.**

- **God made Christ to be sin for me that I might be made the righteousness of God in Christ.**

You say, "Jesus was made sin for me, so that God could make me righteous, and now I am the righteousness of God in Christ Jesus. I am righteous. I'm in right standing with God. We're in union. We're together. There's no distance between us. I am the righteousness of God in Christ Jesus!"

- **I am the righteousness of God in Christ.**
- **I am a worker together with Him.**

Every one of these is from Scripture. You can find them in the Bible of course, but you can find them in the New Man Manual on page 62.

"I am a worker together with Him." I work with Christ. I work with God. We work together.

- **I will glory only in the cross of Christ and what it has accomplished.**

- I will glory only in the cross of Christ. I will glory in nothing I've done. I will glory only in the cross of Christ, what He has done, and what it has accomplished.

- By the cross, the world is crucified unto me, and I unto the world.

- In Christ, only the new creation means anything.

- Jesus has created one new man, and that new man is in union with Christ.

- I am a new man in complete union with Christ.

- I have put off the old man and his lifestyle.

- I am renewed in the Spirit of my mind.

- I have put on the new man which is created in righteousness and true holiness after the likeness of God Himself.

That's what you look like inside.

- There is neither Greek nor Jew, bond nor free, but Christ is all and in all.

- I am buried with Him by baptism into death; therefore I walk in newness of life, because He was raised in newness of life.

- I serve in newness of spirit, not in the oldness of the letter.

- My love is made perfect, and I have boldness in the Day of Judgment, because as He is, so am I in this world.

- I abound in everything, in faith, in utterance, in knowledge, in all diligence, in love for the saints, and in grace.

- I abound in everything, in faith, and in utterance. I abound in knowledge, in all diligence, in love for the saints, and I abound in grace.

- I walk in the flesh, but I do not war after the flesh. My weapons are not carnal, but mighty through God to the pulling down of strongholds, casting down imaginations and every high thing that exalts itself against the knowledge of God, bringing into captivity every thought into the obedience of Christ.

I want you to understand this. If you don't have the New Man manual, get the *Acknowledging What's In You* booklet and CD or MP3. Play it over and over again. Play it when you're driving. Speak along with it. Say it. Say it. Say it. Keep on saying it.

You say, "Are you one of those that does a confessional?" "Yes, I am, most definitely." I'm renewing my mind, and you must renew your mind. One of the ways to do that is by constantly reiterating to yourself what the Word of God has said.

Don't think, "Well, I just don't know what I'm going to do for money. I don't know what I'm going to do if I lose my job."

You have not lost your job, but you're worried about what would happen if you did. "Well, I don't know what I'm going to do if I lose my house. What are we going to do if everything just falls apart?" No! Don't think like that.

Just know that the Scriptures of facts and truths that the Word of God says about you is a reality in you now. At some point you're going to have to decide: "The world can do what it's going to do, but I am going to follow God. I'm going to do what God says."

You say, "People are going to think I'm strange." So what if they think you're strange when you're healed, blessed, prosperous, moving on with God, and not worried about the things of the world? That's who you're supposed to be. You are not supposed to be under bondage of this world or the things in it. We are to be in charge of this thing. Jesus left us here, on purpose, to be in charge.

- **God has given me the Spirit of wisdom and revelation in the knowledge of Him, because He has already blessed me with every spiritual blessing in heavenly places.**

"God has given me the Spirit of wisdom and revelation." You need to say that. Some people need to say it more than others, but you need to say that.

- **The eyes of my understanding are enlightened, and I know the hope of His calling. I know the riches of the glory of His inheritance in the saints.**

- **I know the exceeding greatness of His power toward us who believe.**

Say these things out loud. As you say, "I know these things," then your spirit will start to feed into your mind so that you actually understand. You will start to realize that you do know all of the things the Bible says. You will know these things in your spirit, because you have the mind of Christ. As you start to say these things, it will almost be like those old coffee pots that percolate. It will start to bubble up into your soul, and your soul will get hold of it.

- **God raised Jesus from the dead and set Him at His own right hand. He has seated me with Him far above all principality, power, might, dominion, and everything that has a name.**

Let's just take a second look here. Notice: "The same power He exercised when He raised Jesus from the dead." That's the power He's using in you. It's the same degree of power that He used to raise Jesus from the dead. That power is at work in you, right now! How in the world can you possibly think that problems, situations, sickness, disease, and all of these things can have any type of effect on you?

Do you realize Lazarus died? He didn't die of good health. Something killed him, and he died. Jesus went to his tomb, but He didn't question anything. He just said, "Lazarus, come forth." Whatever power was used to bring Lazarus forth had to raise him from the dead first. It also had to heal him, because if it hadn't, he would have been raised up and just dropped back dead again. The disease would have killed him again, so the power that raised Lazarus from the dead also healed him as it raised him from the dead.

That was Jesus exercising power. After Jesus was killed, God exercised the greatest power in the existence of history. He used that much more power to raise Jesus from the dead. He raised Jesus, who raised and healed Lazarus at the same time. I hope you see this progression.

God used the highest degree of power ever to raise Jesus from the dead, and Jesus bore all your sickness and diseases. They were all upon Him because of His stripes. All of that was taken care of when God raised Him. Imagine the power it took! It was the most power ever used! The power it took to raise Jesus from the dead healed all of your diseases and healed everything that was upon Him by His stripes. That much power is at work in you as a believer, right this second! Right now!

How can sickness or disease live in your body? How in the world can it live there when you have the utmost power? There is no greater power in existence than what is at work in you, right now. This is who you are. This is what is going on inside of you.

The problem is that you say, "Well, my body feels this." Do you know why? It's because you've not renewed your mind to allow the power of the Spirit to flow out of your spirit, through your soul, into your flesh, and throughout all of you. That's the only reason. Once you get hold of that, once you realize Who is at work in you, and once you agree with it, all of that stops. The enemy has no place in you anymore. He will still try to convince you to get sick, so you have to realize Who is at work in you.

It says, "God used that power to raise Jesus from the dead, and He set Him at His own right hand." Now watch this: when He raised Jesus, you were raised with Him. You were put in a positional place with Him, and He was seated at the right hand of the Father, "far above."

Notice what being seated means: "Far above all principality, and power, and might, and dominion, and every name that is named." That's where Jesus was seated, "Far above all principality, and power, and might, and dominion." In other words, there is nothing above Jesus, except God the Father. He's next to Him.

All sickness, disease, poverty, fear, anxiety, depression, all of the principalities, power, might, dominions, demons, and everything else is all beneath Jesus' feet. You are seated with Jesus, because you're His body. That means that all of these things are beneath your feet.

Romans 16:20,

> 20 And the God of peace shall bruise Satan under your feet shortly. The grace of our Lord Jesus Christ *be* with you. Amen.

You need to understand that He's going to bruise Satan under your feet. Why? That's where Satan is! He is below your feet. You are above principalities, powers, might, dominion, and all these things. You're seated with Christ. Everything is below you. Why? That's because it's all below Him. Get your mind off of you, and just realize where you're seated. You are seated at the right hand of the Father, in Christ. The same power that raised Jesus and put Him there is at work in you, because you're in Him.

If the power is working in Him, it's working in you. Why? That's because you're in Him, and your life is hid in Christ. You are in Jesus, and you are mixed with power, in Him. It's all in there, mixed together.

- **God has put all things under His feet, and He has made Him to be the head over all things to the church.**

- **I am His body therefore all things are under me. His Name is my name. Everything that has a name has to bow its knee when I use the Name above all names.**

Do you hear that? Your name is now His Name. You are one with Him, and because of that, when you use that Name, everything that has a name has to bow its knee. That's obviously not the Father, not the Son, but it is you. You're in the Son, so everything has to bow its knee under you.

- **I am His body, the fullness of Him that fills all in all.**

- **Christ is the end of the law for righteousness to me, because I believe.**

- **The righteousness which is by faith talks like this: the Word is near me, it is in my mouth, and in my heart. It is the Word of faith, and it is what I speak, because I am righteous by the faith of Jesus Christ. I speak faith. Faith is what God has accomplished**

through the cross of Christ. I have faith that He has accomplished His will in my life.

That's how faith, which is by righteousness, speaks. There is a faith which is not by righteousness, and that's a faith which is by works. That faith which is by works says, "Because I've been good, then God gives me these things. Because I sow, then God will see that I get it back." That's faith, which is by works.

Faith, which is by righteousness, says, "Because Jesus died at the cross, now I get the benefit of it; because of what He did, I get to reap the benefits."

I'm not saying that you don't do works. The Bible says we are created unto good works, and there are good works that are foreordained that we should walk in. The difference is that the works we do now, we do because we are righteous, not to be righteous. The works we do, we do because we're supposed to do works. There is nothing wrong with good works.

A lot of these unknowledgeable "pseudo theologians" think that all works have to do with the works of the Law; they do not. There are works of faith, and works of faith please God.

If you try to use works to gain salvation, that's a whole different thing. Everybody would agree that it's not right. We don't get things by works, and we don't get saved by our works. We are saved because of what Jesus did. That's the key. However, once you're saved, you're supposed to work. You should do works out of gratitude toward God. You don't do works to be accepted; you do works, because you're accepted. You need to differentiate that.

All of those other things are a part of that hyper-grace thing that's going on. It is ridiculous. I used to call it hyper-grace, but I started calling it heretical grace, because it's to a point where people say, "Oh, you don't need to do anything. Anything you do is a work, and you shouldn't do it." That's a lie! You should do works. We were created unto good works.

- **I confess with my mouth that Jesus is Lord, and I believe that God has raised Him from the dead. I am saved, healed, delivered, and blessed.**

- **I am in a better covenant, made with better promises.**

- **I am Jesus' disciple.**

- **He has put His laws into my heart; I know the Lord.**

- **He is my God, and I am His child. I walk in Him, and He walks in me.**

- **He calls me child, and I call Him Father.**

- **The New Covenant is in force, and the old covenant is gone.**

- **Jesus is my High Priest. He established the New Covenant with His blood and His body. His blood is better than the blood of bulls and goats. His blood remits my sin. His blood removed my sin, and He will never bring it up again, because He has forgotten my sin.**

These are all statements you can make.

- **The law had a shadow of things to come, but never made anyone perfect. The blood of Christ has the reality of being made perfect, once and for all.**

- **I am sanctified through the offering of the blood of Jesus Christ, once and for all.**

- **Jesus sat down waiting until His enemies be made His footstool.**

- **I am His body, His enemies are under His feet, and they are under my feet, because I am His body.**

- **By one offering, He has perfected forever them that are sanctified.**

- **I draw near with a true heart in full assurance of faith; my heart has been sprinkled from an evil conscience.**

- **I do consider others and provoke them unto love and to good works.**

Our job is to provoke one another to love and to good works.

- **I assemble together with the saints, more and more often.**

- **I know that a man is not justified by the works of the law, but by the faith of Jesus Christ. I am justified by the faith of Jesus, and I look to His good works, and not my own, for righteousness.**

- I am dead to the law that I might live unto God.

- I am crucified with Christ, nevertheless I live; yet not I, but Christ lives in me, and the life I now live in the flesh, I live by the faith of the Son of God, who loved me, and gave Himself for me.

- I received the Spirit by the hearing of faith and not by the works of the Law.

- I began in the spirit, and I shall remain in the spirit.

- I live by faith.

- Christ has redeemed me from the curse of the law, being made a curse for me. He was made a curse in my stead, in my place.

- The blessing of Abraham has come upon me through Jesus Christ, and I have received the promise of the Spirit through faith.

- The promises were made to Abraham and to Christ, not to many seeds, but to one Seed, Christ. I am in Christ, therefore, I am in the Seed to Whom the promise was made, therefore, I receive the same promise, the same Spirit as Christ.

- The promises were made to Abraham and to Christ, not to many seeds, but to one Seed, Christ. I am in Christ therefore, I am in the Seed to whom the promise was made, therefore, I receive the same promise, the same Spirit as Christ.

There are pages of these that we go through in the New Man Manual on page 62. The New Man Seminar is geared to renew your mind to who you are in Christ.

As I said before, depression is never God's will. We can break the spirit of fear over you, but the only way for you to get out of it is for you to change your thinking. Think on things that are good, and pure, and holy, and of good report. Put your mind on God, and keep your mind on Him, and you will stay in peace."

Let's go back to Hebrews 13:5,

> 5 *Let your* conversation *be* without covetousness; *and be* content with such things as ye have: for he hath said, I will never leave thee, nor forsake thee.

Be content with what you have: for He hath said, 'I will never leave thee, nor forsake thee.'

Let us pray:

"Father, I thank You, and in Jesus' name, Your Word does not return to You void, but it accomplishes the thing where unto You sent it. Father, this Your Word, and it tells us who we are in You, right now, as a current reality. Father, I thank You that Your Word has gone out, and that those under the sound of my voice in any way, whether they're listening or watching right now, if they are of You and born of Your Spirit, that right now, Your Word is ringing true in their spirit, and they know that the things I've said are absolute truths.

Right now, Father, I thank You that these truths, as they begin to stir up the things that are in them, will become reality, and that their minds will be renewed to the Word of God, that their lives can be transformed, no longer conformed to the earth and the world system, but transformed to look like Jesus, because we were predestined to be conformed to His image.

Father, I thank You that this is taking place, even now in Jesus' name. Holy Spirit, right now, with every believer that has heard these words, I say, 'Begin to work in them, and as You do, work with the Word to remind them and to stir up their remembrance.' I thank You for bringing to remembrance all of the things You've said, all of the things that Jesus Himself has said, and all that has been spoken about in the Word of God.

I thank You, right now, that these things are coming to fruition in their lives, and they shall come to pass. I thank You that the people are being transformed, even now, to look more like Jesus.

Right now, in the name of Jesus, I speak to the people, and I say, you were healed, past tense, 2,000 years ago by the stripes of Jesus, and it is a current reality now. Even now what's been going on in your body has to cease. It has to cease, right now. Pain, sickness, disease, elements, mental anguish, and depression all have to go, now! Every bit of it has to go NOW!

The key is to get your mind stayed upon Him. Get your mind stayed upon God, and He will keep you in perfect peace.

Even now, I say to those who are listening, 'In the name of Jesus, be healed. Be free. God wants you free. For freedom, Jesus has set us free. We are to walk in that freedom. Whom the Son sets free, is free indeed, completely and totally.'

In Jesus' name, I'm telling those people, 'The devil no longer has any call, any rights, or any claim upon your life.

Right now, if you're born of God, and if you have made Jesus your Lord, your sins are forgiven. They're gone! Don't bring them back up. If you don't bring them up, God never will, so don't bring them up. If anyone tries to bring up anything from the past, don't go around them. Get away from them. Stay away from them. Be around people who inspire you and people who put the Word of God into you. Be around people who believe in the best in you, people who bring the best out of you, and people who encourage you and stretch you in the things of God, and go forward.'

In the name of Jesus, right now, I set you free, in spirit, soul, and body. You are free to be free. For freedom He has made us free, so be free to be free! Amen. You are free to be free. We release you from the snares of the devil. Right now, in the name of Jesus, we command your body, Be healed! Function correctly! Do your job! Even now, I say, Mind, I command you to operate in a sound mind. You have the mind of Christ. Mind of Christ come forth!' We ask in the name of Jesus.

Right now, we bind and break all the power of the enemy. Depression, Go! Anxiety, Go! In the name of Jesus, I set them free. Cancer, leukemia, emphysema, tumors…go, in Jesus' name! Loose them now! You cannot stay in these bodies and in these minds. In the name of Jesus, I set you free.

God bless you. Be healed. Be free, in the name of Jesus. Amen."

JGLM Trademarked Names

All derivatives of JGLM names are Copyrighted trademarks:

Divine Healing Technician(s)
John G. Lake Ministries
John G. Lake Healing Rooms
John G. Lake's Divine Healing Institute
Dominion Life International Apostolic Church
Dominion Bible Institute

All derivatives of these names are Copyrighted trademarks and may not be used without the express written permission of:

John G. Lake Ministries
P. O. Box 742947
Dallas, Texas 75374
www.jglm.org

Please advise JGLM if you come into contact with anyone using the following names without authorized permission:

John G. Lake Ministries
John G. Lake's Divine Healing Institute
John G. Lake Healing Rooms
Divine Healing Technicians Certified
DHT

Appendix A: Historical Information

1. The information presented in this book is for historical purposes only. References to people, organizations, professions, etc., are presented for the sole purpose of giving an accurate overall understanding of the prevailing viewpoints of particular groups, religions, denominations, and movements of the time periods referred to in the seminar.
2. Each reader is expected and required to make personal comparisons and decide for themselves which viewpoints to accept and endorse.
3. The material presented and its successful application is predicated upon the viewpoints of those during the time periods in which they lived.
4. Curry R. Blake and John G. Lake Ministries are in no way responsible or liable for the successful application of the material or for future re-presentation of the materials presented in this book.

Appendix B: Practices Concerning Medicine Or Medical Treatment

1. All information presented is not to be construed as advice or instruction in activities or practices concerning medicine or medical treatment.
2. The author of this book is not in any way a trained medical or psychological professional.
3. Any ministry services are being rendered from a position of compassion and mercy and are not to be construed as medical treatments or as substitutions for medical treatments.
4. No one can present themselves or anyone under their guardianship for ministry, without relinquishing and waiving all legal recourse that would or might be the end state of such person and/or anyone they present for ministry.
5. Anyone using this material cannot hold JGLM liable or responsible for their personal practice of ministry.

APPENDIX C: RULES FOR REPRODUCTION OF JGLM MATERIALS

1. The physical material in this book is and shall remain the property of the presenter and the JGLM organization they represent. All material in this book shall belong to the author.
2. No reproduction of the material in this book is allowed without express written permission from the author of this book.
3. Any material and/or information in this book or gained during the seminar or from audio/video material from the host organization, if presented to others at any time, shall be presented in its entirety as it is presented in this seminar, without change, adaptation, omission or addition.
4. Prior to the presentation of this material to any other persons, groups, and/or organizations, reader will contact and inform the presenting organization of personal intentions in writing. If told not to present the information, such person(s) are not to present it.
5. In the event said person is given permission to present information, they are to provide the host organization with an audio/video recording (in its entirety) of the material presented.

APPENDIX D: NON-MEDICAL ADVICE

1. The information presented in this book is in no way intended as advice or instruction concerning the use of medicine, medical treatment, or the avoidance thereof.
2. Each person is responsible to investigate all methods of remedy they are contemplating.
3. No one has a right or responsibility to make your decision except you.
4. Any reference to medicine or medical treatment is solely for historical or informational purposes.

- You are left unsatisfied by the status quo...
- You know you were meant to be a participant and not just a spectator...
- You ask "Why not?..." more than "Why?"...
- You believe that today can be better than yesterday...
- You know you were meant to walk among the Giants of the Faith, and you want the tools & training that can make it happen...
- When you hear the exploits of God's Generals, you can picture yourself doing them...

If this describes you, then you ARE JGLM... whether you know it or not.

COME. LET'S CHANGE THE WORLD.

LIFE†EAM®
The Saints Army

lifeteams@jglm.org

Go out into all the world. Preach the gospel, heal the sick, cast out demons and make disciples

New Man
This Changes Everything...

The Primary focus of the DHT seminar is to train believers to biblically and effectively minister healing. The purpose of the New Man seminar is to reveal to believers what was accomplished by Jesus for us through His death, burial, and resurrection. The New Man Seminar reveals what you are (in Christ) not what you will some day become. It also reveals how to begin being who you are rather than emphasizing waiting for the next "Christian Fad".

An International Apostolic Council Church

Church Membership Requirements

The following email address will be used to communicate with everyone that considers themselves a part of this church.

dliac@jglm.org

Becoming a member of IAC Church:
1. Must confess Jesus as Lord and that you are saved/born again.
2. Must at least be seeking and expecting to be filled with the Holy Spirit in accordance with Acts Chapter 2 (speaking with other tongues).
3. Must agree with the JGLM/IAC Statement of Faith.
   (obtain by emailing us at: dliac@jglm.org)
4. Must be a certified DHT or working toward certification: contact us by email at dliac@jglm.org to find out how to become a certified DHT or you can look it up on our website (www.jglm.org)
5. You maintain communication with us on a regular basis
   (this can be through email and/or physical letters).
6. You agree to pray for us according to the prayer directives that we will send to all church members on a regular basis.
7. You agree to support the church through tithes and/or offerings.
   Tithes and/or offerings must be sent to the PO Box not to the church address and MUST be memo'd as Tithes/offerings:
   PO Box 742947, Dallas, Texas 75374.

1104 Summit Ave. Suite 102
Plano, TX 75074

Dominon Life Church

John G. Lake Ministries
Same Message. Same Power. Same Results.

DOMINION BIBLE INSTITUTE

TRAINING THE NEXT GENERATION OF GOD'S GENERALS

SIGN UP TODAY!
dbi@jglm.org